Lana Bataineh, better known as "Loofy", is a mother of three who was leading a relatively healthy life when, at the age of 44, and out of seemingly nowhere, she was diagnosed with Amyotrophic Lateral Sclerosis (ALS). The disease takes away the patient's movement abilities and eventually works its way to the lungs, causing respiratory failure. The disease is considered to be fatal within two to five years from the time it is diagnosed.

Now, 16 years later, Loofy has overcome the medical statistics and is thriving. In this book, she talks about her journey to healing, and how she was able to mentally stop the fatal spread of the disease. Beyond finding stability in her physical condition, she has managed to inspire countless lives along the way and now uses her platform to help others get through their struggles.

To my precious family. I am blessed with the most loving and supportive family one can ever imagine. The unwavering love and devotion we have for each other has been the driving force behind my battle with this disease.

Lana Murad Bataineh

CHOOSING LOVE

AUSTIN MACAULEY PUBLISHERS™

LONDON • CAMBRIDGE • NEW YORK • SHARJAH

ISBN – 9789948452225 – (Paperback)
ISBN – 9789948452218 – (E-Book)

Application Number: MC-10-01-3155373
Age Classification: E

First Published (2021)
AUSTIN MACAULEY PUBLISHERS FZE
Sharjah Publishing City
P.O. Box [519201]
Sharjah, UAE
www.austinmacauley.ae
+971 655 95 202

Prologue

When I first started my blog, on which this book is based, never in my wildest dreams did I think that it would reach so many people from all over the world. It started as an idea put forward to me by my youngest son, Karim, to express my thoughts and feelings. It was confusing to me why anyone, apart from my family and close friends, would be interested in my thoughts, *ha ha*.

From the very first post I wrote, the reaction was overwhelming and with each piece of writing, the readership kept growing. This response was truly life-changing. It opened up new doors for me; I started expressing myself and reconnecting with people after living in silence for so long.

Through my blog, people have gotten to know me better and understand how my family and I are living, coping, and striving with Amyotrophic Lateral Sclerosis (ALS). It has helped people understand that living with this disease is not a death sentence, it is a choice of living and making the best out of a difficult situation. My blog has become like therapy to me; knowing that my articles inspire some people has been motivating me to keep writing. Being told that my blog has helped make someone feel less alone is so rewarding; it is a form of healing and cleansing of the soul.

I have received comments from people all over the world saying that I have helped them in some way. It is so exhilarating to realise that my words have the power to inspire so many, and that they can help people who are going through a rough time. Knowing these stories is also inspiring to me, and helps with my healing process; it is very therapeutic and humbling. I am so grateful to now be sharing my story in this book, and thankful for the support I have received from all my readers.

My dearest readers, your comments and kind words have served to motivate and encourage me. This confirms to me that I am relevant, and, despite my inability to speak, I am heard.

Thank you once again.

Me

I am not much of a talker these days, but believe me, I have lots of interesting thoughts circulating inside my head and I am excited to invite you all in. I am living with ALS and have been for 16 years now, which has rendered me incapacitated. It has taken over every muscle in my body, except for my mind and spirit – those still belong to me. In fact, with every physical muscle atrophying, my spirit has grown in strength.

ALS is a form of motor-neuron disease that essentially stops your muscles from receiving messages that your mind is sending. It is also known as Lou Gehrig's disease. There is lots of information online that a quick Google search could tell you about the disease. However, seeing as I have the privilege of speaking for myself, I would like to describe it to you in my own words.

If you look up ALS on the Internet, it will tell you "degenerative disease… life expectancy three to five years".

The reality is that it first affected my legs: without warning, they stopped responding to the orders being sent from my brain. I would be walking then, suddenly, I would stumble in a very weird way. Slowly and progressively, my legs started to get heavier and heavier, as if someone had strapped weights on them, so I would have to drag them slowly. It was a very strange and scary feeling.

Gradually, I started losing my balance, I would need someone to hold my hand, and support me in order to get from point A to point B. Just like that, I lost my independence and my life would never be the same. I would have this frightening image of me confined to a wheelchair, and found myself praying night and day that the dreaded image would not come true.

Unfortunately, however, it did.

I used a cane, then a walker for a few months, then the wheelchair. Sitting in my wheelchair for the first time was probably the second worst day of my life, after being told that I had ALS. It felt like I was given a life sentence, it was such a gut-wrenching moment that I shall never forget.

I had to learn patience, tolerance, acceptance, and perseverance like no other time in my life. All that while trying to come to terms with the fact that ALS is a hurricane going through my body, killing every muscle it comes in contact with.

Then came part two of the disease: losing the use of my arms and hands. At first, my fingers started to cramp up, rendering my hands useless to me. Then, my arms started becoming heavy objects attached to my torso but absolutely useless. They were like two heavy logs of wood that I had to carry around in my wheelchair. This phase was particularly difficult to accept, naturally because it meant that I was now completely dependent on another human being in order for me to function.

Finally came the third and most devastating attack: my voice. I was silenced; my ability to communicate was stolen away from me, leaving me trapped in a useless body with so many unspoken words in my mind.

ALS takes its toll, not only on the body, it also drains you emotionally, leaving you raw and sensitive to your surroundings. It is like drinking all the water from your well of life, and, if you are not careful, it can be the end of you. It is an attack on your patience, your tolerance, your passion, your emotions, your family, your hopes and dreams, your livelihood, and your faith.

This motor-neuron disease has affected me deeply in some ways that neither books, articles, nor doctors tell you about. It took away my dignity; I had to accept drooling in front of everyone and see how they looked away so as not to embarrass me, which was even more embarrassing. It took me so much time to accept eating in front of anyone. I had to start being fed like a baby, with food coming out of my mouth. On a baby it is considered cute, but on a grown up, it was the definition of humiliation. It took every ounce of strength to learn how to accept and adjust to these awkward new life accessories, wearing bibs or having tissues under my chin constantly.

These are just some of the visible struggles we have to accept as patients of ALS; I shall keep the embarrassing hidden battles attacking my dignity as a grown woman, such as being taken to the bathroom or given a bath, to myself. Nowadays, I am happy and proud to say that I have learned to live with all these adjustments. I no longer feel ashamed, or embarrassed; in fact, I feel happy and grateful that I am still around, bound to a wheelchair, drooling and being fed, but alive and thriving.

Happiness is a choice and I choose to be happy. Circumstances do not define my happiness; instead, my soul and mind are the driving forces behind it.

Since I became ill, the scale by which I measure happiness changed; I became much more appreciative as to what is important in my life. My sense of values also shifted – I realised that I was searching for happiness outside my home, but I was looking in the wrong place while it was inside of me all along.

The first step to experiencing happiness was acceptance. Once I learned to accept my situation, I found serenity and peace that I had never felt before. In an almost contradictory way, my illness became a blessing for myself and my family. With acceptance came contentment. Being content, I think, was the key that unlocked the door to my joy. Learning how to be appreciative and grateful for the little, simple things in our life that bring us serenity is priceless. I had to accept my limitations, and seek to find satisfaction within myself and within my home. My home became my new surrounding and although I spend lots of time alone, I am never lonely.

These days my happiness comes from my family, I am motivated by my love for them, which is the greatest, strongest fuel for life; if they are in good spirits then that is more than enough for me. I experience life vicariously through them. I feel their joy in so many ways; if they are having a good day, then that is reflected on my own day. I also find happiness in compassionate gestures; a kind word, or an unexpected kiss (wink) *ha ha*. Happiness is being surrounded by friends and family, it is a visit from one of my sons or daughters-in-law, even a simple video-conferencing session with them. Happiness is giving back, it is being told I am inspiring, or helping somebody in need. It could come from listening to a good song, or having a good meditation session. Happiness is waking up with no pain and a good night's sleep.

I might miss some activities in my life like walking, talking, or even just feeding myself, but that does not define or dictate whether I am happy or not.

Many people might think I am suffering, but believe me I am in a very good place. I look around me, count my blessings, and realise I have so much to be grateful for. I am at peace, I am content, I have found my serenity, and I am happy.

*****

People often ask me and wonder how I function on a day-to-day basis. I am, and always have been, a master of routine. I wake up late, around 9:30 am, due to the fact that I have nowhere to go, and I am my own boss *ha ha*. While still in bed, I meditate for 10 to 15 minutes, then I get up and first of course, check my phone just like the rest of the world. I then have a plate of fresh fruits, followed by my breakfast while watching TV. The reason being I am a very slow eater, so instead of staring at a kitchen table, I entertain myself. Also, I tend to make funny noises while attempting to swallow, so the noise from TV muffles these sounds, and deflects from the mess I make while eating, just like a baby in a high chair, *ha ha*.

I then go to my Eyegaze computer, which is an assistive device adapted to my capabilities... or lack thereof. Eyegaze is a computer that uses eye-tracking technology to assist with my communication, it has a camera attached at the bottom of the monitor and is pointed towards my eyes. On the screen, it has a standard computer keyboard, which allows me to type by simply looking at the letters. My eyes then work as the mouse; all I do is simply look at a letter and it types it. Then, I look at the speak button and the computer speaks whatever I type. It's amazing!

There, I reply to my messages. Most important is touching base with my family, I make sure I am sending them happy, positive vibes for the day. I check my blog, and emails, then give out instructions to my caregivers – what to do, and what to cook, check what shopping we need, make shopping lists…etc. Just like any housewife.

Then my caregiver wheels me into my room in front of my closet where I pick out my clothes for the day, then into my bathroom for my daily shower. After I am dressed, I do my daily physiotherapy exercises. I then step into my office again, where I sit around one to two hours on my computer replying to my emails, working on my blog and attending to Facebook and Instagram.

Most days my beautiful sister, Tammy, comes during this time, and we are able to sit and chat on my Eyegaze computer. Sometimes I have friends, or family come to visit me, they know I finish my physio, and am ready for visitors around 12:30pm.

Often times, I love going into the kitchen to supervise the cooking and do some major tasting with some minor adjustments. I then have my daily salad followed by lunch, again, while catching up on my TV shows or while watching sports – I love watching tennis, especially Roger Federer, I am a huge fan of his. In fact, meeting him in the winter of 2019 was one my lifelong dreams which came true.

Around 4 pm I retire to my room for at least two to three hours. I nap, meditate again, and catch up on my reading. I listen to audiobooks on my iPad, followed by another batch of physiotherapy exercises, to keep my joints and limbs flexible.

By then, it is around 7pm in the evening, and I would either have friends and relatives coming to visit, or I log onto my computer to chat with my husband and do some work. Due to my inability to speak anytime I want with my husband, I have to type out everything I want to say to him during the day, and then speak to him all at once when he comes home from work. I usually prepare my points of conversation like a board meeting, *ha ha*. I do not like bothering him too much, especially that he has just come in from the office, but I have no other choice. At least he gets his peace and quiet once I log off my computer, *ha ha*.

After my evening session on my computer, I run out of energy. So, I just sit in front of the TV with dimmed lights, to rest my eyes as they tend to get very tired from using my computer. I have my dinner, watch TV until it is time to sleep, thankful to have successfully managed another day. I sleep, wake up, and repeat the same every single day.

You might ask "don't you get bored?" For sure I get bored, and lonely sometimes, I am human. But I have learned to block these feelings, and replace them by filling my days with activities that I am able to do, and forget about what I cannot do.

I am very strict with my daily schedule, and try my best to adhere to it. I do this for two reasons; first, and most importantly, that system has proven to work well for me health-wise over the years. I managed to stay stable for many years, *Hamdallah*[1]. The second reason is that it is much easier for my caregivers to take care of me when there is a daily routine.

It is truly a blessing for which I am continuously grateful. There is not a day that goes by that I do not acknowledge the fact that as an ALS patient, I remain one of the rare, lucky ones that has survived and thrived for so long despite living with this debilitating disease. I am living proof that leading a healthy lifestyle, being organised, keeping busy, and having a positive attitude can result in so many happy days.

Some of the things that bring joy to my life, which people might not know about me, include hosting friends and family.

---

[1] Translated as 'Thank God,' this phrase is often used in conversation, especially when thanking God for blessings

I love entertaining people. Sometimes, when my husband or sister are out of town, people ask about me and say they would love to come visit but never show up. I get disappointed when that happens – why would you say that if you did not mean it? I understand that life gets in the way, and that is totally fine. Simply do not promise to come if you cannot make it.

It might also surprise people to know that I do most of my shopping by myself, online shopping that is. I even ordered my dresses for my son and nephew's weddings online. I also love grocery shopping so you can imagine my excitement when this option became available in Amman – where I currently live. I miss the luxury of choice, to actually look at options of a certain product, as opposed to being forced to buy the same thing over and over again.

I love being asked my opinion, even if it is just to humour me, *ha ha*, my kids are specialists in this field. I dislike being the last to know something, or forgetting to be told about anything. It is quite infuriating being treated as if I do not exist. It is true I do not participate in whatever is happening outside my home, but it is nice to be considered, or at least be treated as if I am not invisible.

I am a strong advocate that despite being "sick", I should always make sure I am presentable. You will never see me without my hair done, or without my nails and toes perfectly manicured and pedicured in the summer. That is not to say I am vain, or that I have diva tendencies, *ha ha*. It simply makes me feel good about myself as I would have done when I was healthy. When it comes to makeup, however, I only put it on for special occasions so that I shine, except for a little daily lipstick or lip gloss to distract from my drooling (secret trick).

My faith is one of my guiding forces, I still pray five times a day, despite not being able to physically pray or perform the washing for prayer (ablution). I just have the "intention", I close my eyes and pray on time. I never once questioned God "why me"? From the beginning, I was convinced in God's wisdom and mercy. That is why I was, and still am, hopeful. Spirituality always played an important role in my life, but when I was first diagnosed with ALS, I reached a dead-end when my doctors told me: "Sorry we have nothing to offer you, there is no cure, goodbye." At that point, I was left with no choice but to dig deep emotionally, mentally, and spiritually. You will be surprised how much comfort and solace I found.

There is a whole new world, of spiritual and mental help out there just waiting to be picked from the tree of life, all you have to do is reach out and believe. I found so much help that enabled me to survive, and thrive, but my cup is overflowing with strength and positivity that I am able to help others.

*****

Although I consider myself optimistic, there are certainly many challenges I go through as well.

First of all, I miss a lot of things. Apart from the obvious – talking and walking, I miss hugging my family. A good hug is taken for granted; I miss the heart-warming feeling I get when I squeeze them. You never realise how precious some things are in life until you cannot have them.

I miss eating popcorn. It used to be my favourite snack of all time, but now it is a dangerous choking hazard for me. One time, Karim, my youngest son, tried to make popcorn then crush it in the food processor for me, bless him. Great idea but the taste was not the same – the crunch under my teeth, bursting the flavour in to my mouth was missing.

I miss reading, it used to be my relaxation technique and my way to gradually fall asleep at night. So Zeid, my eldest, introduced me to audiobooks. Now, I listen to books faster than most people can read, *ha ha*.

I miss kissing my children, so Faisal, my middle child, makes sure to press his cheeks on my lips to remind me how sweet they taste. Since I cannot purse my lips anymore for a kiss, that is the closest feeling to a kiss these days. I love it when Faisal does that.

I miss exercising, I used to be one of the very first people in our area to practise soul cycling (we used to call it spinning classes back in 2003). It was a very intense workout with great music, and a lot of fun! It is a great way to release all your negativity, tension, and aggression, and replace it with a cheerful mood.

I miss eating a simple hamburger, a small hot dog, or even a juicy shawarma, remembering how its juices dripped onto my hands. Some meals are finger licking good but, unfortunately, I am unable to enjoy some of them; I cannot hold, bite, or swallow these meaty meals anymore.

I miss speaking in Arabic; all my speech is done through my assistive computer, Eyegaze, which only speaks in English. There is a lot I want to say on certain occasions, like a certain Arabic saying or phrase, but it just has to remain swimming inside my head with no escape; it is frustrating at times.

I miss driving – I used to love the freedom of getting in my car, music playing full blast, and I would sing along to my favourite songs, like Nancy Ajram or Celine Dion, while driving myself to work. Speaking of singing, oh how I miss singing to my favourite songs, or dancing – my husband Marwan and I used to always be the first and last ones on the dance floor at parties!

In addition to all those things, I also had to go through some drastic changes in my life due to being confined to a wheelchair, and my fashion style has been one of them.

Like most ladies, I used to have my own sense of fashion, I was quite stylish if I might say so myself. Due to having lost control over moving my legs while sitting, I am unable to close them just like a lady should, *ha ha*, and so I have had to give up skirts and dresses, especially short ones (which were my favourites) and instead substitute them with trousers. My trousers must be the elastic waist kind, without buttons and zippers, in order to be able to put them on while sitting down and, also, for maximum comfort while sitting for long periods.

As I gradually started losing the ability to move my arms, wearing shirts and jackets were also eliminated from my wardrobe, as they required certain movements of the arms to put them on, which I was unable to do. My tops also have to be of a stretchable material, like wool or cotton, in order to put them on with ease. The biggest challenge has been putting on a jacket, or God forbid a coat! It is absolutely impossible unless it is really loose, and even then, two people need to be helping me.

I also had to make sure my sweaters have a low cut as high cut sweaters or turtlenecks would not work, due to eating difficulties and continuous drooling. Because I lost control of my neck area and mouth, I have become a messy eater, *ha ha*.

Another adjustment which I had to make was of course my footwear. I have had to give up heels or any elegant feminine shoes and replace them with practical ones such as flats and slippers.

One day, I looked at myself in the mirror and I did not like what I saw – I felt like I was dressed like a much older woman! That is when I decided to do some changes to my style; I might be sick, but my spirit is still young!

From that day onwards, I have been buying only colourful clothes. If you open my closet now, you will find it is like a rainbow of colours. I discovered that wearing colours, as opposed to wearing black or shades of grey, is very uplifting to the spirit. Now you will see me in happy sunshine yellow, or funky fuchsia pink, clear sky blue, vibrant orange, or flowery prints – anything that makes me happy :). My elastic waist trousers are no longer dull colours, they are either flowery, or with any other fun pattern. As for my shoes, they also got an upgrade – in the summer I wear colourful fashionable sandals, with perfectly manicured toes, and in the winter, well, sensibly warm but colourful slippers, *ha ha*.

It all comes down to your attitude towards any situation, if you are given lemons, make lemonade. Being confined to a wheelchair, does not mean you cannot be stylish.

I was dealt a hand that did not allow me to dress as I wish, so I made the best by wearing colours, it brightened the way I looked, and put some much-needed boost to my mood.

Despite all these challenges, I remain thankful and truly grateful to be alive to see my children progress and succeed in their lives. I hear from them what things taste like, feel or look like; I experience the world through them.

*****

Being a patient suffering from a debilitating disease is definitely a scary thing. Becoming motionless and speechless has meant that I had to face new fearful situations that I was not prepared for.

I have a fear of being left in a room on my own with the door closed. Once, I was left alone by one of my home therapists who often comes to help with my meditation, which left me scarred. They had finished my session, walked out of the room, closed the door, and went home without telling anyone. I could not shout – because I was afraid, my throat closed up and I could not make a single sound. My body then went into spasms due to the tension and stiffness. With every minute that passed, I would get worse until finally, one hour later, they checked on me – everyone thought my therapist was with me. Since that day, I am petrified of closing my door.

I have a monitor connected to my caregivers, so when I wake up, I just make a sound into the speaker for them to come check on me, it must be close to my mouth or else nobody can hear me. I am afraid of waking up one day and needing assistance, and finding a broken monitor disabling me to communicate with them.

I am afraid of choking on Sundays, you might think 'why Sundays?', it is because that is the day my caregiver has her day off. She is the only one that knows exactly what to do when I am choking. I am also afraid of needing emergency medical assistance while my husband is travelling, his work often takes him out of town.

I am afraid of getting stuck in a locked car with the key inside. On the days I venture out of the house and they place me in the car, they always close the doors while packing my wheelchair because it is cold, but that scares me as these days, cars are programmed to lock themselves. *Ha ha*, okay maybe this fear is irrational but it is still a thought that crosses my mind.

I am also afraid while flying that the plane might need to make an emergency landing, at which point I cannot go down an emergency shoot, or put on a life vest or swim. I am not afraid of the actual emergency on flight, it is my inability to react that scares me. When traveling and staying at hotels, I am afraid of the fire alarm going off, because if a fire breaks out the first thing that shuts down is the elevator, meaning that there is no way down and out for me. Again, I am not afraid of the actual fire, it is my helplessness in that situation that scares me.

Naturally, I have much more serious fears about complications in my health deteriorating down the road, but I made a promise to myself not to think these thoughts and to delete them every time they creep up. That way, God willing, these serious scary conditions from ALS might not happen to me. If you believe in something strong enough it becomes a reality, *Insh'allah²*.

I think admitting and facing our fears head on is winning half the battle. It is very courageous to admit our fears, but once you confront your fears you will find it very therapeutic.

Besides these new fears created by my disability, I have also had to learn to adjust to living in silence. Have you ever heard the lyrics of the famous song by Simon & Garfunkel, "The Sound of Silence"? *"People talking without speaking; people hearing without listening; people writing songs that voices never share, in the sound of silence."*

That is how my world has become. ALS has condemned me to a life of silence by taking away my most vital organ – my voice. Leaving me drowning silently in an ocean full of speech and communication of which I can hardly participate in. The silence can be so frustrating, and depressing if I allow it to take control of my feelings, leaving me quite lonely.

---

² Translated in Arabic to "God willing". It refers to events that one hopes will happen in the future.

I have been living in silence for over thirteen years now (three years after I was first diagnosed) and that has affected me in many ways.

For instance, when sitting with someone, be it a friend, relative, or a family member, they would be talking and all I can do is simply shake my head for "No" or blink my eyes for "Yes". I miss having a conversation, or participating in an ongoing one, although I do join in, but only silently in my mind. I miss voicing my opinion when something is being discussed. I have so much to say about everything, I am a very opinionated person, *ha ha*. But again, I am forced to let my points silently float in my head without anybody hearing them. Sometimes, I have to wait until the next day (when I am on Eyegaze) to weigh in my two cents on a certain topic if it is important enough, but most of the time it just passes by in silence, and what I have to say is no longer important.

I am so silent that most of the time people forget to talk to me; everybody talks, discusses, argues, and challenges each other while, as time passes, they forget that I am in the same room even, making me feel invisible. I do not blame them, I completely understand that in order to be considered, I must be an active contributor to an ongoing conversation. So, I find myself sitting in silence. I could be in a room full of people, but I might as well be alone. It hurts to be treated as irrelevant.

Laughter is a release for the body, it is well known that your body releases endorphins which act as a mood boosting agent, which I have been deprived of. I have a sense of humour, and just like everybody I enjoy a good laugh. However, even my laughter has been silenced. When I laugh, no sound comes out, and everybody thinks I do not get the joke but, believe me, I am laughing on the inside, I just have difficulty expressing it.

Same applies to when I am singing; I love singing, I used to fill the house with my voice while cooking, or doing my chores – much to the annoyance of my children, *ha ha*. Unfortunately, now I sing along in complete silence. The other day I went to see "Mamma Mia!". All my favourite Abba songs were playing and all I could do was shake my head in utter silence; but, inside my mind, I was singing every word, and enjoying myself.

Sitting in complete silence, I continue to talk to the wall, and sing to the ceiling, and laugh at the floor. Despite being silenced, there is so much going around in my brain, from discussions, to singing, laughing and joking but the difference is that nobody can hear me.

*****

We are all unique humans who react differently to each circumstance. I was 44 years young when I was diagnosed with ALS and given two to five years to live. I recently celebrated my 60th birthday.

Being stable is a miracle in itself, which I am so grateful for. I wake up each morning with gratitude filling my heart after a good night's sleep. I wake up and find myself breathing naturally, pain free, and full of life. My blood tests all show that I am healthy, apart from having ALS, *ha ha*. I do not have high blood pressure, high cholesterol, and no deficiencies of any sorts. That is wonderful and, I believe, is a good reason to celebrate. God blessed me with good health to keep fighting my disease. Good strong body and mind making me forget I am sick sometimes.

Some people do not like to celebrate their birthday and would rather nobody remind them of it because they do not want to admit they are getting older. Before I became sick, my birthday was never a big deal, but since then everything concerning me has changed. Celebrating my birthday has now taken a whole new meaning for me; It has become a time to celebrate life and the joys and blessings that come with it. It symbolises a significant milestone for me. It reminds me to be grateful for witnessing another year, and to be thankful for achieving another victory in the battle with ALS, *Hamdallah*.

When I reached 50, I really started to be grateful for birthdays. I wanted to make sure my 50th birthday was a day to remember. It was such a huge milestone for my family and

I. We made sure to celebrate how precious life is and be grateful for the extended time we have with each other.

Since then, I make sure to celebrate my birthday, as each year is a reminder that I am winning this battle, and gaining so much wisdom, faith, peace, tranquillity, and serenity. Which had led to my contentment and happiness.

ALS has reshaped how we think, adapt, and function as a family. But, at the same time it has taught us valuable lessons in life, and shone a light on what really matters. For sure, the experience enriched our life with attributes like no other family has. This has become our family badge that we wear with pride, it is a barometer of which love and hope can be measured by; it is the definition of love motivating me.

When I think of my mother, I think of her smile.

It was late August 2005, the end of summer, my mom had been living with ALS for over a year at that point. My two older brothers, 18 and 21 respectively at the time, had wheeled my mother into my grandfather's room and closed the door to have a conversation. We had been staying at my grandfather's house whilst spending the summer in Amman.

It was the afternoon and I, 15 at the time, was sitting on the steps at the edge of the garden. If you have been to Amman in the summer then you would know just how delightful the weather can be at that time of year – especially in the afternoons. The sunflowers, the little bushes, and the garden lilies were all warmly nodding back at the low, setting sun. The pink sky was reflecting the blissful calm mood in the garden – which was in direct contrast to the turbulent storm gusting inside of me.

I was thinking, how I will handle being the only child in the house for the first time? My brothers were preparing to set off to college in the U.S. (one for his 3rd year and the other for his first.) I was left thinking, How will I take care of my mother?

Over the past 12 months I had seen my mother go from a healthy, active person to being confined to a wheelchair, with very little ability to move. The deterioration was rapid, confusing, and painful.

Until that very moment I was protected. I was allowed to be a teenager, sheltered from the harsh realities of life. The reality which my family found itself in, and that was that my mother had a life-threatening disease (ALS). I knew enough to understand she was sick, and I could see her physical condition rapidly deteriorating day-by-day, but until then I was offered the privilege of not having to face it. That privilege, however, was now gone.

In the middle of that haze, in that beautiful Amman afternoon sitting at the steps of my grandfather's garden, I was thinking of how I was going to face my mom after she comes out of the room with my brothers. I knew they were saying goodbye as they were headed to the airport in a few hours and I remember feeling, for the first time in my life, that I was not ready to face that situation. I had no frame of reference to rely on. I could not think of one word to say, or even a gesture to make. I never thought something so confusing could be so gut-wrenching at the same time.

I was hoping that door would never open.

My mother was never one to keep her feelings hidden, whether it was letting my basketball coach know how she felt about benching me, or crying while watching a sad movie. Goodbyes, in particular, were not her forte. So I had every reason to expect her to be an emotional wreck. That terrified me, as I had nothing in my arsenal to console her.

Sometimes, you experience a situation that even though you do not fully understand it at the time, you intuitively know the intense magnitude of it all – like a tectonic shift taking place underneath your feet. The scene I saw in front of me once that door opened was my family's own tectonic shift. The golden door handle moved and the door made that unnecessarily loud noise it makes once it is jerked into sudden motion. My vision was so focused on my mother that I have no recollection of even seeing my brothers, who flanked either side of her wheelchair, emerging from that room.

As my eyes scrolled up, I saw my mother seated as she normally was in her wheelchair. The wheelchair had black cushions, red metal support railings, small wheels (it was a pushchair, so no need for those large rear wheels). My mother was seated with her feet relaxed on the cushioning at the bottom, arms rested by her side. I continued to lift my gaze until I saw it – it struck me and took a hold of me, of all of us, for as long as we will live. A beautiful beaming smile was painted across her face from ear-to-ear.

It was a smile that came from a place of conviction, from a place so deep within her soul, a smile so pure that its genuineness implores you to smile along with her. A smile full of confidence that says: "I will survive this disease no matter what." In that moment, the ominous clouds inside me departed, leaving me awash with a feeling of peace.

I now understand that my mother in that moment chose to live. She made a conscious decision to do what she has always done, lead us to a better life. I now understand that it was at that very moment my mother chose to put an end to being sick, and chose to begin healing -her medicine? Her beaming smile. Her choice trickles down to all of us and laces our every decision with positivity towards a more peaceful way of living.

It is now 2021 and we are preparing to celebrate yet another birthday for my mom, her 61st and 16th with ALS. In those 16 years my mother's smile has continued to shine in power and conviction. Her ever-growing inner peace and happiness spreads to all of us. I am now in my thirties, a much more grown-up version of myself from the sheltered teenager I was 16 years ago. I understand I have a lot of growing up to do, many challenges to overcome ahead of me. However, with my mother's fighting spirit serving as a constant guide, I can approach my future (and present) with courage and measured optimism.

– **Karim Bataineh,** Lana's third and youngest child

Family

My life was sailing along peacefully until suddenly, a storm blew in an illness that came crashing through the door into my home, and changed my life forever. It transformed me from an energetic, healthy human being, actively participating in life, into a spectator watching it go by from the stands, unable to take part in the game of life.

In the beginning, my health was deteriorating at a rapid pace. I had never heard of ALS before, so, like everyone else nowadays, I rushed to the internet to find out more about this devastating intruder. One sentence kept appearing in every article "life expectancy is two to five years". I went into denial, I refused to read anymore, I refused to listen to stories, or watch programs. I shut the "life expectancy" subject off completely and started visualising that my life was going to go on and on. Denial is an emotional reaction to bad news but, when merged with hope, it became a powerful weapon that gave me ammunition to fight my battle against this beast, which we then came to know as ALS.

As my symptoms increased and my health got worse, I felt like I was losing control of my life. I found myself desperately searching for love; I wanted to touch and be touched, hug and be hugged. My life became more meaningful, and my time with my family became more precious so I turned to them and, looking into their eyes, I drew hope and strength.

This unforgiving news did not only affect me, it also turned my whole family's life upside down. Our lives changed drastically; we huddled around each other, we became closer than ever before and our life started having more depth and meaning than we could have ever imagined.

It made us better humans. We appreciated life and valued each other. I love life so much that I found myself clutching at it with all my heart. It is the love that I have for my family and the need to be a vital part of their life that gave me the will to fight in order to witness how their lives shape out. More than anything, I want to stick around, and be there for important and memorable milestones in their respective journeys.

Life is an exploration in search of the ultimate happiness which, unfortunately, eludes most of us. We spend most of our life searching in all the wrong places. We chase wealth and measure our success through it, we collect material things instead of accumulating spiritual wealth and peace of mind. We waste our time thinking that the grass is greener on the other side, inevitably making us miserable.

We must treasure contentment in our life in order to achieve true happiness. Thanks to our unfortunate circumstances, my family's life has become enriched with meaningful love, happiness, and appreciation. After all, "it is not how you die, it is how you live".

I was told by top specialists at Johns Hopkins 16 years ago to get my affairs in order. My first thought was, *Oh my God! I will not be around to witness and be part of all these significant moments in my children's lives*. Little did the doctors know that a mother's determination and love can perform miracles that science is unable to explain.

As a mother, you dream of certain occasions in your child's life from the day they are born. First steps, first word, first day of school, first game played, first school exam, graduation, first job, and then, their wedding day.

One of those milestones in my family's life came on July 15th 2016, my first son's wedding night. I did not just take part in the wedding; I was involved in every single function. I helped organise it, I ate in it, and I even danced in it. I also watched my son take his beautiful lovely bride for their first dance, I witnessed the sparkle of love and joy in his eyes, I was there for the happiest night of my life.

Another one of those amazing milestone moments came 3 years after that, on August 2nd 2019, when I attended my second son, Faisal's engagement to his beautiful fiancée Zeina Rifai. I am extremely happy, blessed, and grateful to have been part of my sons' happiest days. I never thought that God would allow me to be part of these festive occasions in my children's lives, but then again that is why I call this a miracle. Dream big, have faith, reach for the stars, pray hard with belief and, most importantly, never lose hope, for God will reward you. I am reaping the benefits of my patience by dancing at my sons' wedding and engagement parties, in a wheelchair, and first one to hit the dance floor.

In both occasions I felt like I was floating, like I was in a dream, like my feet were dancing although they were glued to my chair. I felt like I was clapping to the music despite my hands being paralysed, I felt like I was singing despite my inability to speak, I felt like I was dancing with everyone, except that I was watching from a distance. I felt like I was a sponge absorbing my sons' love, and witnessing the joy in their eyes, while looking into their future wives' eyes. I was overwhelmed with feelings of joy, pride, and love for my family like no other day. I was happy!

I know you might say that every mother feels extremely happy at her son or daughter's wedding. However, when you have a terminal illness and you are able to overcome all odds when they are stacked against you, then that is an extra spectacular, wonderful feeling of achievement and accomplishment.

Saying this is a dream come true for me is an understatement. Every mother dreams of the day when her son finds the perfect partner to spend the rest of his life with. I have been praying since the day I found out that I cannot take care of my three sons anymore. Praying that they will find a partner who can carry the baton from me, in nurturing, caring, and unconditionally loving my sons. Ensuring their happiness is one of the most important things for me.

*****

I feel fortunate to be surrounded by an incredibly supportive family, starting with my caring and loving husband, Marwan. Since my diagnosis, he has been by my side in every step of this journey. Never wavering, continuously lending his love, support, and optimism. He always makes sure I am well taken care of, providing me with the best equipment for my comfort while being my best friend, my confidant, and my companion. Talk about taking the marriage vows 'in sickness and in health' to a whole new level. How can I give up my fight when I am blessed with such a wonderful man?

The love and support I get from my children is my biggest motivation. I have three wonderful young men: Zeid the eldest; Faisal is my middle child; and my youngest, Karim. There is also Zeid's lovely wife, Reem, and Faisal's beautiful fiancée, Zeina, all now living in Dubai. Despite them being far away physically, emotionally they are extremely close. They have the ability to make me feel like I can conquer anything that comes my way.

My love for my family is the driving force behind my perseverance to hang around for a very long time. I believe they deserve that I give them my best, simply because they are the best.

Their words run through my veins, nourishing my soul and giving me the strength to believe that I am invincible. It is their daily dose of love and encouragement that propels me forward to keep dreaming and hoping. How can I give up my fight after receiving such incredibly motivating and strengthening words?

I feel that I am one of the luckiest people on Earth. Despite my boys being so young and inexperienced at the onset of my disease, my family has always been extremely supportive and protective of me from the beginning. They were there for me every step of the way, which has pushed me to be there for them always.

We were living in Bahrain at the beginning of my illness. I loved going to the beach, so my boys would carry me to the water and dip my feet in the sea when I first lost the ability to walk. Our roles in life were reversed; they became the protective mother, and I the child. They would cut my food, spoon feed me and wipe my mouth when I first started losing the use of my hands. You might think, "Oh, how sad…" but I would say, "Wow! How beautiful."

When I felt like I was going to lose my ability to speak, I would sit them down and talk to them as if there was no tomorrow. I would give them advice on life and how to conduct themselves as gentlemen. Bless their hearts, they listened carefully and, like sponges, they soaked up every word. I would see how eager and attentive they were, which left me searching for more power to find ways to make me stronger in order to motivate them.

My family's tender loving care towards me is proof that I am needed as a mother, as a wife, and as a human being. They are so attentive; despite working and living in another country, they always find time for me throughout their busy schedules and they make sure they are involved in every detail concerning me. They are experts in making me feel relevant – which is a vital component to my strength. My boys never once made me feel useless. On the contrary, up until this day, they come to me for advice and value my opinion in matters concerning their lives.

I love being useful, I love being considered, I love being a mom. It is an absolute necessity to feel needed when hit with this disease, because ALS robs you of every single task of being human. That is, if we allow it.

Being an ALS patient, it becomes very easy to feel invisible; people start visiting and asking about you less, and some might not bother with you as much as you would like them to. All these things happen not because they do not care, but simply because you lost the ability to function or communicate like a healthy person, leading to feelings of despair and melancholy. However, my boys manage to compensate for any void I might feel with their continuous love, dedication, and attention. ALS has taken my ability to walk and talk, but has blessed me with the realisation and appreciation of what really matters in life.

My support system is not limited to my husband and boys; my beautiful sister, Tammy, also plays a vital role. Those who have met Tammy know what a caring soul she has. Although she leads a very busy life of being a devoted and loving wife, a mother to three children herself and maintaining a social life. She somehow always manages to find time to check up on me and take care of my needs.

My illness has left me somewhat isolated from society (for better or worse, *ha ha*), but Tammy always makes sure I am never lonely. She pops in to visit me almost daily, armed with her warm loving heart and big smile. She is my angel who brings the outside world into my home. She always informs me of what is trending, who is getting engaged or married, what new restaurant opened, whether it is good or not, or where to get the best food delivery from. All the mundane everyday bits of information that people might take for granted, but Tammy knows I need to hear or I would be out-of-the-loop so to speak.

Bless her *habibti*[3], she is also my personal shopper – she always makes sure I am aware of where the latest sales are happening (I always love a good bargain, *ha ha*). She either goes to the shop to take photos of the items on sale, ranging anywhere from furniture to napkins, and sends them to me to choose from. Sometimes she also takes me shopping – who does not love shopping with their sister? It does not stop there – she also takes me to go visit my friends. It is the little activities that might not mean much on the surface, but mean the world to me.

Tammy embodies what family unity truly is. She makes sure family traditions are never forgotten; she loves any activity that brings us all together; she has become a mother figure to our family, despite her being the youngest sibling.

I do not know how I would manage without having Tam Tam in my support group; she gives me love when I need it, she gives me compassion when I am missing it, she gives me

---

[3] An endearing term in Arabic widely used to refer to loved ones.

understanding when I feel misunderstood, she is my sounding board when I am angry or frustrated. She is always caring, loving, and nurturing not only to me, but to my whole family. To be honest, everybody's life would be better with a little Tammy in it, *ha ha*! She is my best friend; she is my sister.

*****

Motherhood is the ultimate blessing we receive from our creator – at least I believe so. Holding my child for the first time opened the floodgates to new, beautiful emotions that shook me to my core. There was no way I could have a bad day after being blessed with motherhood. Hugging my baby washed away every negative thought and replaced them with loving, positive, beautiful thoughts. There was so much love that poured from my heart in that instant, that it redefined what love meant to me.

Becoming a mother gives you powers that defy normal explanations. Just the sight of any one of my children can make the day seem like the happiest day ever. I might have the weight of the world on my shoulders, but a look or a smile from one of my children will make me feel as light as a feather. The joy and happiness motherhood brings is unmatched; as females, we are so blessed to be born with these maternal instincts of unconditional love and an unequivocal devotion that separates us from most men. I am not diminishing the feelings of fathers, simply stressing the feelings of mothers.

Motherhood is giving without wanting anything in return; it is about dreaming, hoping, and praying for someone other than yourself. It is about wanting happiness, love, success, and good health for your child more than you have ever wanted for yourself. From the moment I became a mother, I found a new purpose in life – to nurture, love, and care for someone. Like never before. In return, I was rewarded by being happy and blessed in ways I was unaccustomed to as well.

I am willing to go to the end of the Earth just to ensure my children's happiness. Loving them is so rewarding and fulfilling; it is what fuels us as mothers to sacrifice everything just for our children's comfort and well-being.

Karim is my youngest child, my baby, but he is every inch of an amazing young man. I know every mother believes her child is special, *ha ha*, but Karim has a heart of gold – he is such a kind, giving, and loving soul.

Karim had just turned 15 when I got the devastating diagnosis that I had ALS and that there was no cure for me. Naturally, as a mother, my first instinct was to protect and shield him from worrying that he was about to lose his mother, so I hid some facts about the seriousness of my condition from him; in fact, I hid it from all my children.

My fear of not being able to see him graduate from school, be there for his first day of university, or help guide and support his decisions in life shook me to my core and left me feeling helpless and frustrated. I was overcome with fear, but thankfully, God had other plans for me. Not only did I attend Karim's high school and undergraduate graduations, but I also got to witness him graduate from his Master's program a few years ago. I believe in miracles so that's why I plan to be around for future milestones in his amazing life, trust me I still have a lot of fight in me.

Karim is also constantly participating in different fundraisers with the ALS Association, hoping to find a cure for me – bless him, we are such a hopeful family. He is always encouraging me to try new activities to cut down on watching TV, and to read and write more. In fact, it was his idea to start the blog, and, subsequently, to write this book.

*****

Faisal is our middle child, his nickname is Fox, but I call him my blue-eyed Fox, *ha ha*. Since the day he started talking, he became the entertainer in our family; he would act out his storybooks with sound effects, putting on a show for anyone who would watch. At school, he would always participate in the talent shows, either acting or rapping. The performer in him transitioned into sports – whether he was playing basketball, football, or baseball, he would always put on a show. Luckily, this helped him in his line of business: he is an engineer in the oil and gas industry, and he is very comfortable in front of an audience when delivering his presentations and illustrating his charts and graphs.

Faisal brings so much joy to our family; he is responsible for all of our nicknames. He is constantly analysing situations in a very funny way and finding witty remarks for everything. He has the ability to roll back the fog and part the clouds revealing clear blue skies for me, constantly showing me the silver lining in any tough situation.

Most dear to my heart is that he always finds time for me; he is always in tune with me, my life, my needs, and my feelings. Faisal is always thinking of what I need in advance: if we are going out somewhere, he always puts my mind at ease; he is my planner and facilitator and always does it with so much care and love. He solves my problems, big or small; he would ponder, rub his chin, and bite his finger while thinking, then come up with a solution, my Mister-fix-it.

Recently, Faisal found the love of his life and life partner, Zeina. She is beautiful, sophisticated, sweet, kind, and loving. She makes my son extremely happy, and therefore has won our hearts collectively as a family, and individually she booked a permanent place in my heart from the first day I met her.

Zeina's family has unfortunately suffered a great deal of loss in the past due to the passing away of her beloved mother, and the passing of her stepsiblings' father. However, they found a way to merge their grieving families and create the perfect, happy, loving, caring family. It is a lesson on how to convert a negative situation into a positive one, a lesson on how to turn despair into hope. I believe in my heart that is one of many reasons Faisal and Zeina fit so well together; they both come from families that have found a way to appreciate what matters in life through hardship.

*****

Zeid is my first born, and, like any mother will tell you, there will always be something special concerning your first experience with motherhood. From the day he was born, he has been my Zeido, and he will remain Zeido no matter how old he gets, *ha ha*.

Pursuing his long-lasting passion for Yoga, Zeid spent some time in an Ashram to become a yoga instructor. During his time there, we would always Skype and I witnessed a beautiful transformation in my son. He became much more zen and tranquil. It seemed like he had discovered the key to his happiness. His philosophy is accumulating life experiences as opposed to accumulating actual things in life. I am so proud of his choices and the way he values his ideas and beliefs.

Naturally, all parents want to see their children happy, but we must learn to allow them to choose the path they wish to follow, even if that path is different from our choice. Our job is to encourage and support them to follow their dreams and their heart. We must remind ourselves that each generation has its own set of beliefs and ideas. We can dish out our advice, help guide and point out potential pitfalls that they might encounter, while trusting them and respecting their choices.

It is during this serene period of his life that Zeido found his soulmate, his beautiful wife Reem. Seeing them both so happily in love is such a blessing, and has given me so much joy and peace of mind.

Reem, or as I like to call her "Reemo", came to visit me in Amman for a week. We sat for hours talking, getting to know each other while communicating on my Eyegaze. We watched chick-flick movies, had amazing meals together, joked and laughed, and even went out for coffee. We enjoyed each other's company just like any mother and daughter would. The more I get to know her, the more I fall in love with her; Reemo has such a beautiful, sweet soul.

Sometimes, I try and join in a conversation, or voice an opinion by spelling out a word, but it is very difficult for people to understand me. Reemo, bless her, was determined to learn how to communicate with me, and find a way to understand me. For an entire week, she showed such genuine care and determination to understand what I am trying to say, and how to take care of me, all the while being so attentive to my needs. From the minute she arrived, she started recording on her phone a video of how I spell every letter in the alphabet, and what gestures and movements I make for certain needs. She created a tutorial video, which she would study all the time, so that by the time she left, she could understand me. This is the sweetest, most compassionate thing anyone has ever done for me.

I was touched beyond words by the love and kindness I was shown. The willingness to invest the time and effort in finding a way to understand me is heart-warming. For that reason, I felt like I was touched by an angel.

Reemo also gave me the most incredible gift a parent could ever dream of: a grandchild, Ghaia.

*****

I expected the birth of my first granddaughter to be something special, but I could not fathom just how wonderful it would be, and how our new bundle of joy would lift my spirits.

It is a whole new level of love, just as strong and deep as my love for my children, yet different in the sense that it is a beautiful extension of love that sprouted from my heart. A love I was told to expect but could not imagine, a love that serves as a new motivation for me.

It is God's will that due to my health condition I was unable to attend my granddaughter's birth. It is at times like these that I find it extremely hard to accept my situation. Frankly, I abandoned all my positive attitude and fell into self-pity. It was painful to come to terms with the fact that I would not be available for this momentous occasion. My happiness and anticipation were overshadowed by negative thoughts of feeling sorry for myself until the very moment she came into our world. Her parents sent me her picture right after she was born and it was like a rainbow appeared amidst my dark cloud and brightened my life. It was a reminder of what really matters, and a very cute reminder at that.

I felt like my whole body erupted with pure love and happiness, like an overflowing fountain gushing up to the heavens. The minute I saw her face in the picture I felt like the angels were ushering this precious bundle of love into our lives, bringing us renewed hope and purpose.

Who would have thought that I would make it to see my eldest son become a father? I know happy tears flow from every new grandparents' eyes, but, for me, may I say it was a heart-stopping moment. I felt thankful for a natural, uncomplicated delivery, grateful for a healthy baby, and overwhelmed with feelings of immense joy and happiness for my son and his beautiful wife who will get to experience the pure unconditional love of becoming parents. Most importantly, I felt grateful to be alive to witness this day, a dreamed reality that almost slipped away from me.

Having been told sixteen years ago to go home, get my affairs in order, prepare my children and say goodbye to them, you can get a sense of how miraculous it is for me to become a grandma. I believe in miracles, I believe that I am living proof of that: a miraculous grandma if you will, *ha ha*.

Shortly after she was born, I got to spend a lot of time with my granddaughter, getting to know her. I would wake up to see her lovely face and hear her beautiful cooing sounds every morning. It filled my days with excitement and motivated me to get out of bed every day. I would feed off her early morning energy – nothing compares to a baby's positive vibes in the morning, it is contagious and heart-warming.

It is amazing how something so simple like looking out my window and seeing her laundry hanging out to dry became an enormous source of joy – the little dangling pyjamas or palm-sized T-shirts always brought a smile to my face. I could not physically bathe her, but I got to see and enjoy her daily bath as well. She would sit in her chair beside me every day and despite not being able to talk directly to her, I would talk to her through my computer and recite nursery rhymes and tell her how much I love her. I felt like a real grandma, well sort of!

Although it saddens me knowing I will never be able to physically be a grandma: I will never be able to pick up my grandchildren, or wrap my arms around them and hug them. I can never feel the joy of feeding them and bathing them like grandmas are supposed to enjoy. However, I will compensate for that by loving them more, by setting an example for them on how to become a strong person and woman. I can show them what unconditional love is. I can be the grandma that has so much to say and without being able to speak. You can bet I will be that grandma with all the candies and chocolates they will sneak into my bedroom for, *ha ha*.

It is funny because I do not remember myself as a child but I clearly remember my mom Lana and it is through her that I can form a picture of my childhood. Whether it is our Tajleed[4] sessions at the start of the school year, or her coming back from vacation with suitcases full of the latest and coolest gear for my brothers and I, or her belting out the Bee Gees and dancing around our house. She is front and centre, crystal clear, in every memory. She is especially present in all my sports memories, which played a massive part in our childhood. Football, basketball, baseball... you name it. She was always there, be it for practice, Friday morning games, school tournaments, or friends coming over to play basketball for hours. I remember her waking us up in the middle of the night to watch the NBA playoffs. Sports really was a corner stone in our family and a huge part of our upbringing.

I remember the beige suit too. You see, my super mom Lana was president of the Amman Little League and part of her presidential duties meant that she gave speeches and awarded trophies at the end of each season. I clearly remember this one beige suit she would wear. She would stand tall on the podium and give speeches with a loud and clear voice (ironic) that exuded confidence.

I am ashamed to say that the clarity in my memories of my super mom Lana started to get murky around the same period when she got sick. Perhaps it is murky by design, like a shielding of some sort. It is fascinating how powerful the human mind can be and how it can warp reality for self-preservation in order to achieve what must be achieved. I

---

[4] Tajleed is the Arabic term for lamination. In this case, it is referring to the process of laminating schoolbooks at the start of each new school year

believe that is a very important truth that our family's story is filled with.

I honestly cannot point to the exact moment, but I remember that my super mom started getting sick and changes began happening. I vaguely remember conversations with my dad, with all of us huddled together talking about these changes. I remember when I actually decided to read about ALS and how one sentence in particular stopped me in my tracks every time and I could never finish the articles: it read "fatal in two to five years". That sentence did a number on me. I cried a lot those nights. I just could not grasp it and the more I tried to read, the more that sentence came up, the more desperate I felt. The more I cried.

One time, Mama Loofy came back from one of her "medical trips". Just as we were getting in the car to leave, mom's jaw locked up, there was a sound and then her jaw unjammed. This was a new change, on top of the reduced mobility. At the time I really did not think much of it, but damn that memory hurts now. See it actually symbolised this whole damned disease. This disease was churning in her body, taking her abilities one by one. The jaw thing was the beginning of her slowly and painfully losing her ability to speak. Just like everything else this disease takes slowly, cruelly, and mercilessly.

Sometime in this murky period, there is one memory that I will never forget and that is clear as day. It was one night in Bahrain, mama was sleeping, or trying to at least. At this point, she had already lost most of her ability to move and it was in the early stages of losing the ability to speak. That night, she was really struggling to communicate to her caregivers what she needed. It was probably something as simple as itching her nose. But I sat there feeling helpless as she was struggling to communicate her pain. I will never forget that night, I did not sleep at all. I cried a lot that night.

Looking back at it now, I think that was the bottom because something happened that night. I decided to always keep my door open when sleeping in that house (my room was beside my parents'). I started praying in bed every single

41

night from that point onward for a very long time, I would pray and beg in the most creative ways my mind could muster for a cure or for relief for my Mama Loofy. My memories actually seem to get clearer from that point onward.

I remember having deep spiritual conversations with a lot of different people – Muslims, Christians, Buddhists, atheists, yogis, you name it. Very fulfilling and soul nurturing conversations that really broadened my horizons and enlightened me. At the same time, I started noticing mama focusing more on spiritual healing and less on medicinal physical healing. I witnessed first-hand those positive energy signatures shielding her and slowing her decline until eventually it put the brakes on that damned disease's progression and brought it to a halt.

I always needed to understand how and why things work. I just cannot accept that they simply do. I always loved math and physics, the pursuit of how and why things work, so I guess I was always meant to become an engineer. It is ironic because Mama Loofy's case is the one thing that has no How or Why. To me, that was very difficult to accept, but Mama Loofy made me believe that it is not about the hand you are dealt, it is what you do with that hand. The hand itself is purely random, whether in the case of my mom or of any poor kid born in a war-torn country. That randomness is a key element to this life's simulation, that is the only way to make it fair for the countless souls. It is also the only way I can reconcile my mom's How and Why. I admit, I will never be able to solve it. Doctors and science cannot tell us how she got that disease or why, they cannot tell us how to cure it or how Mama Loofy is still here, beating the medical odds up to this day. This whole journey cannot answer me why she suffers, why she is in pain, why did my super mom Lana have to go through this pain? That inescapable pain she goes through for every little task, every single day. It is the one how and why that as an engineer, and son, I will never be able to solve. But with time, I learned to reconcile and live with it, the same way she lives with her disability.

I believe the measure of one's being is what he or she does with that hand. That is where your mind becomes unstoppable and anything is possible. I have witnessed this first hand with my Mama Loofy. The power of mind over matter, love over reason, and energy over reality. I believe my super mom Lana is a miracle called Loofy, and I am blessed to have been touched by such a miracle in my life.

– **Faisal Bataineh,** Lana's second and middle child

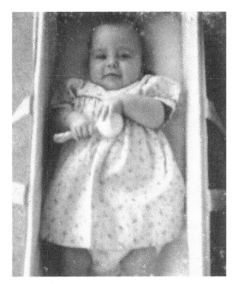

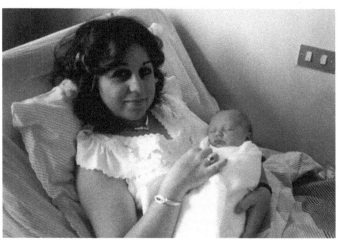

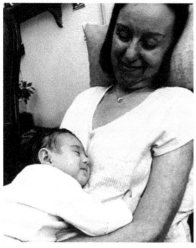

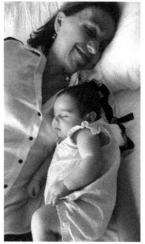

Coping

After I was diagnosed with ALS, my body functions quickly started to deteriorate.

First, I lost the use of my legs. Naturally, I went through a wave of emotions starting with anger, followed by frustration, sadness, and, finally, acceptance. With the help of my strong faith, I was able to remain hopeful and optimistic. Shortly after, I lost the use of my arms. Needless to say, I went through all of the above emotions all over again. But being surrounded by my very supportive and loving family, I was able to persevere and remain hopeful.

One day, I woke up to find out that my voice had changed, followed by days of slurred speech. I knew this would only mean one thing: I was going to lose my ability to speak. My speech started deteriorating, and it was becoming harder and harder for anyone to understand me. Despite digging deep into my faith, I could not find the strength to accept that I could not give advice, share a joke, discuss life, have a conversation, congratulate, or simply say "I LOVE YOU" to my children and husband. As a person, that was extremely hard, but as a mother, it was brutal. Frustration and bitterness were building up inside me, I was sinking, and, at that point, it felt like I had hit rock bottom. Far from being discouraged, it was at this moment that my husband and brother found me the Eyegaze computer.

I typed my first sentence on a warm summer day at my parents' house in Amman. With my whole family gathered around waiting anxiously to see how it would work, I was able to say, "I Love You". I finally had a voice again. With this new voice came immense happiness, new possibilities, and new dreams. From the day it arrived (two years after I was diagnosed), nobody has been able to silence me, *ha ha*.

Fun fact: while I am typing whatever I want to say, I hear my old voice in my head. However, the computer voice comes out very dry and automated – even when I am joking, it comes out serious. This means that I lost some of my sense of humour with the output. Therefore, I named my computer "Diva".

Other than helping me speak, Eyegaze is hooked to my normal computer and, with the use of my eyes, I can control the mouse – from then on, the world is my oyster. I can log on to the internet and function just like any healthy person would, but, because my eyes can only move the mouse one direction at a time, I am much slower, *ha ha*! Having said that, I can type with my eyes faster than most of people can type with their fingers (Speedy Gonzales).

Being able to communicate and perform daily tasks on my own – whether it is emailing a friend or a bank manager – gives me much needed independence. Because I have to rely on my caregivers to do everything else for me, it becomes a treat to do something by myself. A whole new world was further opened up for me when, shortly after I received my Eyegaze, my son Zeid downloaded WhatsApp Web on my computer, which allows me to use the messaging application on my browser instead of on my phone. You might think, "So what is new about that?" Well, to me, it meant being able to communicate with everyone PRIVATELY. It brought me so much happiness. I was finally able to use my own words and choose my own emojis. I was like a kid in a candy store, *ha ha*. Before having this new ability, I used to type my messages on the Eyegaze, which my caregiver would then type up on my phone and send. Now, I can send all my messages on my own and have the freedom to say what I want, when I want.

Freedom, privacy, and dignity are all words that take on a different level of meaning in my world of communication. Having lost my privacy many years ago, being able to have something that is private brings me immense joy and I feel like I got some of my dignity back.

Similar to loss of privacy and dignity, loneliness is also something I've had to cope with. During the early stages of my journey with ALS, my children feared that I would get lonely, as I was increasingly being isolated from society, so they opened up a Facebook account for me. Starting my Facebook page was, and still is, my gateway to the world outside my home – it was both delightful and informative. Today, I am able to catch up with old and new friends – I get to see who has become a grandparent, whose kids have graduated, gotten engaged, or married. Who is happy, who is successful and so on. I am also able to catch up on what is happening in the world and the latest trends. Most importantly, however, I get to voice my opinion, and hear other people's points of view about different topics.

Some millennials might think that Facebook is for bored housewives, but, for me, it is an escape from isolation. It is proof that my opinions and views are heard, that my existence matters, and, more importantly, that I can connect with people, which is stimulating, invigorating, and makes me happy.

My boys then created an Instagram account for me. At first, I was sceptical, I could not understand the concept, *ha ha*. But now, I am hooked on it. Instagram keeps me connected with everyone by visualising what people are doing with their lives. As I am no longer able to stay in touch by having a normal phone call, I can now participate by posting photos, and by having the pleasure of seeing what my friends are posting. From their photos, I get to see the world through their eyes and marvel at the places I cannot physically visit. I also get to see all the summer weddings and functions I get invited to but cannot attend. I especially love seeing family photos of my friends' children and, nowadays, grandchildren and life in general.

*****

If I allow it to, this disease can deprive me of everything, from major bodily functions to small daily-life pleasures.

However, with my strong support network, I have been able to retain some of my joys in life.

I have always enjoyed cooking and making sure I provide good healthy choices for my family. During the past few years however, I found myself having to expand on my variety of recipes as it became a necessity rather than a luxury. Due to the deteriorating muscles in my throat, it started becoming harder and harder for me to swallow certain foods. I found myself restricted to fewer choices of meals, which led to boredom, loss of appetite, and, eventually resulted in weight loss. That was unacceptable for my battle against ALS as I needed every weapon in my body to function to its utmost capacity.

Seeing as I could not go out to restaurants, I decided to bring the restaurants to my home. No, no, not take-out or delivery, *ha ha*. I started following different chefs on the food channels on TV, which I would then record and ask my caregivers to copy these new recipes in a book for me.

The following day, I would be wheeled into the kitchen where we would try to cook these recipes with lots of nodding and shaking my head (and some messy tasting), until we would have perfected the meal. The result: four full recipe books, delicious meals, healthy appetite, and, most importantly, no weight loss! In fact, I gained some weight… *sshhh*.

Eating healthy is becoming increasingly more popular these days, especially with millennials who are so aware of what they put into their bodies; certainly, much more than our generation is. Personally, having been born way before, I learnt a lot from my children and have started to be much more cautious and aware about healthy eating, both for myself and my family.

I need to take a lot of medication for my condition, which can put a strain on different parts of the body. The first thing I did was, as much as I could, to cut down on some of my medication without making myself uncomfortable. I then distributed my medication into five doses over the course of the day. Different meds for different symptoms – some for muscle pain, others for my nervous system…etc.

The trick was to take them with fresh fruits or salads, that way I combined medication, snacks, and healthy portions of fresh fruits. Having to take so many medicines can put a strain on our kidneys and liver, which is the reason behind spacing them over the course of the day. I also make sure to drink lots of liquids to enable my kidneys and liver to flush out any toxins. All these minor adjustments might sound insignificant, but rest assured that they actually contribute to my well-being. Every little bit helps; life is a series of building blocks.

When fighting any illness, it is imperative to watch closely what we put inside our bodies. Certain 'super foods' such as broccoli, cabbage, and leafy greens are more powerful than others and help us boost our immunity and fight diseases, so I make sure I eat those in abundance.

Due to my weak lungs, I tend to eat in small portions because, if my stomach is full it puts pressure on my lungs and my heart-beat becomes faster. Therefore, I always use a very small plate which forces portion control (people who are trying to lose weight should try this helpful tip). Speaking of weight, it is very important for me not to gain too much of it as my gym membership expired over sixteen years ago, *ha ha*.

Unfortunately, there are so many foods that I am no longer able to eat due to my weak swallowing muscles. I miss them, but at the same time I cannot complain, most of my fellow ALS patients are forced to eat through a feeding tube. I am very fortunate and blessed that I am still able to chew, swallow, and digest most foods. This is of course, with extra help from my caregivers who prepares my food with so much care; they cut them up into little bites and add my favourite "extra sauce". I am so thankful and grateful for that, *Hamdallah*.

As you can imagine, I need care 24/7, so it is essential that my caregivers are devoted to my needs. It is not easy to find someone that provides me with compassionate support and empathy but, luckily, I have been so blessed to have two wonderful ladies that I am pleased to call "my angels".

They are my angels sent to me to make my life easier.

They take care of me night and day: they bathe me, dress me, turn me over several times during the night, they help sit me down on my chair and take turns sitting with me while I watch TV to assist in changing the channels. I have a baby monitor connected to me wherever I go, so, when I need them, I simply make different sounds and they come to check up on me. They have become part of our family and a vital part of my amazing support group.

One of my caregivers knows how to feed me with the exact consistency so I do not choke, which is a major hazard for us ALS patients. If I do choke, she knows exactly what to do so that I can breathe. She has become my hands; she brushes my teeth, my hair, washes my face and puts on my make-up (yes, sometimes I actually put makeup on although I do not need it, *ha ha*).

I consider myself extremely lucky and blessed to have them in my life; taking care of an ALS patient requires lots of patience, attention, and empathy. It is very physical and time-consuming, but, thankfully, my caregivers have all the above in abundance. I am so grateful for their continued dedication and commitment. I thank them in my prayers, and during my daily activities. I will always be indebted to them for their continued dedication in caring for me and I cannot imagine my life without their help.

*****

Just like we have four seasons during the year, we go through different seasons during our life. We experience the sunny happy phase, the dull slow phase, the bitter-cold gloomy days, and the energetic flowery phase. We must learn to accept all the challenging moments that are thrown on our path and ride the wave of life. The same way we accept the happy moments, we must also accept the dreary days. We can do this by attempting not to dwell on the low times and always find a way to climb out of our sad or angry moods.

It is surprising that we mostly see happy occasions posted on social media, although being unhappy is as much part of our day-to-day life. Why deny these natural feelings? I believe that accepting and acknowledging the bad times is just as important for our well-being as it is to experience the more upbeat moments. When I started writing my blog, I had promised myself and my readers that I would talk about my raw emotions, as I believe expressing feelings is very therapeutic to one's mind and soul.

There are some days when I feel deep sadness and loneliness, which could be triggered by not being able to travel or attend a relative or close friend's special occasion. Every now and then, I feel a minor setback in my health, which scares me and makes me feel very anxious. But, by far, the most upsetting and what makes me feel extremely frustrated, is when my family members or caregivers show any sign of impatience with me. I get angry and irritated and think to myself, "why are they being impatient"? No matter how hard it is for them, it is ten times more difficult for me to try to be understood. Although, to be fair, it does not happen that often.

I have no problem in admitting my anger, worries, and my genuine emotions. The trick is to accept the anger and frustration and to shift them to forgiveness, patience, and, eventually, happiness. Some people get offended by my display of honest emotions as I tend to be quite blunt sometimes. I think it is much better than bottling these negative emotions inside as they only serve as toxins if not released.

Dealing with my emotions has also taken a new importance with my condition as one of the side effects of living with ALS is that I have become extra sensitive – both emotionally and physically. I have always been emotional, but, these days, my nervous system has made me ultra-sensitive. I shall not attempt to explain the medical condition behind it, but rather tell you how this affects me.

Imagine my body like a box full of electric wires, making up my nervous system. Now picture an electric current running through them all day. Sometimes, the current runs smoothly while other times it is broken, causing intermittent signals from my brain to my muscles. In turn, this makes my muscles twitch and throb, making them shake violently, to the point that you can actually see my skin vibrating. This could happen to any muscle anywhere in my body: one minute it is in my thigh, the next it is in my back, arm, neck, face, hand, chest, or foot. Unfortunately, this constant vibration of the muscles goes on most of the day and makes me feel fatigued most of the time. So, I keep distracting myself from this discomfort by watching TV, reading, working during my office hours, being surrounded by people, or, the best distraction these days is writing.

All this miscommunication in my nerves makes me extra sensitive. If it is cold then I feel extra cold, especially now that I am also immobile. If it is hot, then I feel hotter than anyone else. My body is so sensitive that if I go from one room to another and the room is even 2 degrees colder, my body starts shivering. My body also shivers when I am excited or nervous, so everybody thinks that I am cold. It is confusing, I know, try living with this condition.

This sensitivity has also heightened my receptiveness to sound. Any sudden noise makes me skittish. If the house is quiet and the doorbell rings, for example, I jump and feel the ripple effect through my body. If there are too many people talking at once, I feel like someone is playing the drums inside my head, especially if the TV or radio is also on.

Another funny fact is that when my caregivers sit me down on any chair, I must be cantered exactly in the middle of the chair or else I start leaning sideways like the leaning tower of Pisa (as Faisal calls it) *ha ha*. The same occurs when putting me to bed: I must be exactly in the middle of my side of the bed or else I roll over onto one side. All this is hard for a healthy person to imagine, but I have absolutely no muscles to perform the simplest of tasks, like balancing myself.

You might think I am whining or complaining, believe me, I am not. I am simply stating some facts about how my nervous system is messed up. On the positive side, due to my sensitivity, I get the royal 'handle with care' treatment from everybody; they are constantly checking up on me and asking me: "Are you hot? Are you cold? Are you comfortable? Do you need anything... etc." I am pampered by everyone, and I am always the centre of attention in the room, making me feel very special and loved.

*****

Despite being very sensitive physically and emotionally, I must confess that I feel stronger than most people think. Stronger mentally and with a much stronger willpower to survive and beat the odds that are stacked against me.

I am often asked about some of the mental healing techniques I use. The answer is in my spiritual focus.

After my diagnosis, I found myself becoming more spiritual; apart from my strong religious faith, I started being introduced to different aspects of spirituality like meditation and Reiki, which I now practise on a regular basis. A number of people would come visit me, offering tips to help me cope mentally with what I was facing. I specifically remember one lady who wrote on a piece of paper one sentence: "positive thoughts produce positive results". She then made around 20 copies and distributed them all around my house so that everywhere I turned, I would see this sentence and repeat it in my mind, over and over again. It became my mantra; I would repeat it all day until my mind and body were totally convinced of its power.

I have trained myself to deflect any negative news, whether it is about someone getting sick or, God forbid, the death of someone I know, close or not. The minute I hear any bad news, I immediately replace it with a positive thought and think of something that makes me happy or I remind myself of something that I am blessed with and grateful for. It is a tool that needs practice to perfect. Naturally, receiving bad news is very upsetting, but the idea is to not dwell on negative news, to learn to move on and to immediately replace that image with a positive one. Holding on to sad thoughts will not change the facts, so you might as well go in to a happier state of mind. It is not being selfish; it is being positive.

Surrounding myself with positive images that lead to positive thoughts has worked very well for me. For example, I hang all my children's university diplomas on the wall near my bed. It is the first thing I see when I wake up, and last thing I see when I go to sleep; I call it "our proud accomplishment wall". I keep photos of my family on my bedside table as well as in my living room which is full of precious moments. These images are the happy imprints in my mind.

By creating this positive environment for myself. This has led me to be very content and at peace with my situation.

*****

Apart from the inner adaptations ALS has forced me to deal with, I also had to adjust my lifestyle to accommodate my strained physical capabilities. Leaving my house for instance has become a big ordeal for me: it needs planning well in advance of going anywhere. Aside from the obvious, I need to consider who is taking me? How I am going? How long the outing will be? How many caregivers are needed? Will there be eating involved? It is such a mission, often times ending up as a mission impossible. I end up cancelling the plan all together as it is too stressful to deal with, defeating the whole purpose of going out.

Before I go anywhere, I always need to do a site-check ahead of making the trip. First and foremost, I need to check if where we are going is wheelchair accessible. If the location has only two or three steps, then it is manageable: I can simply arrange for my wheelchair to be carried. Any place with more than three to five steps, however, is off limits for me. Because my body has no muscles to anchor me to my chair, I am petrified of falling off.

As a result, that rules out the majority of the restaurants, coffee shops, and even friends and relative's homes in Amman, Jordan. You might think, "but aren't there elevators in most buildings?" Well, apparently, wheelchairs do not fit in most elevators in Jordan – a minor oversight with building regulations. If everything is okay, I have to pray I do not need to use the bathroom! *Ha ha.* That is definitely wheelchair unfriendly: the bathroom stalls are usually too small to fit wheelchairs.

Being confined to a wheelchair is hard, but being confined to a wheelchair with nowhere to go is a travesty. All the above-mentioned activities can be considered privileged outings which I have accepted to live without. However, what frustrates me the most is attempting to see a doctor or a dentist in Amman. The majority of doctor and dentist clinics here do not have access to wheelchairs – they either do not have ramps, or their clinics are in buildings with an elevator that is too small for any wheelchair. Whenever I have my regular check up at the doctors, I am obliged to admit myself into the emergency ward at the hospital instead. Furthermore, it took me two years to find a dentist that is wheelchair friendly, which was a big ordeal since regular dental check-ups are a necessity for us ALS patients.

I am disappointed at the lack of consideration to the wheelchair community in Amman on multiple levels from urban planning, to zoning ordinances, to building code regulations and I feel obliged to shed the light and bring awareness to these issues. When I finally do find somewhere that ticks all the boxes and you see me out and about, I always have the biggest smile on my face. A smile that shines to deflect the looks of pity and the negativity. A smile that overcomes my inability to speak and says loud and clear, "I am okay. I am so happy and I am out of the house."

Travelling is another enormous challenge for me; I am petrified of so many aspects regarding leaving my comfort zone. Getting on a plane, for example, means dealing with a lot of difficult obstacles. So, does organising my hotel room, which I need to ensure has all my needs taken care of. I get anxious just thinking of all the special arrangements that need to be made to make sure I am comfortable throughout the trip. Fatigue could cause irreversible damage to whatever functioning muscles I have left in my body. It is therefore vital to be well rested before, during, and after my journey.

First, we must obtain special permission for my wheelchair to remain with me throughout the flight. I cannot use the airport wheelchairs as they do not have back, neck, and head support and also do not fit in the cabin. Another problem I face is the bathroom on the plane: due to the fact that there are no wheelchair-friendly bathrooms on any kind of plane, I am confined to flights not exceeding three hours. As you can see bathrooms are a big deal for us ALS patients, *ha ha*.

I take a yearly trip to Dubai to see my kids and grandchild. I call my trip an 'adventure' because Dubai has so much to offer.

I am extremely proud of myself for being courageous to attempt these "adventures". There was a time when I would not dare to leave my house due to fear of experiencing health issues, or of the staring eyes and inquisitive looks full of pity in public places. I personally would prefer a smile.

For me, these adventures are a way to regain my freedom. Freedom means being set free from one's cage, being granted the ability to choose where to go, what to eat, how to go, and when to go. This is what the amazing, wheelchair-friendly city of Dubai offers me.

During my stay there, I have been able to go anywhere a healthy person is able to go. I was able to experience how amazing living in this city feels like as a person with disabilities. For example, a small gesture, which sends a strong message, is how we are referred to as "People of Determination" – I really love that.

People in wheelchairs are treated with so much respect, dignity, and importance – we get VIP treatment everywhere we go. A few examples include having a special line for wheelchair access at passport control upon landing, special entrances at all venues, and wheelchair seats at all events with some even offering free parking for accompanying vehicles. I know it may seem trivial, but it means so much just knowing that someone cares about us, that someone thinks we are special and worthy of a few perks in life. Knowing that someone actually cared enough to provide this freedom of movement for the handicapped community touches my heart to the core, it even reinstates my faith in humanity.

There is also an on-call taxi especially for wheelchairs, the best part about it though is that we receive a 50% discount for the fare – how amazing is that? Not only does the city make sure it is wheelchair friendly, but it continues to encourage people like me to go out and enjoy what the city has to offer. The ability to go everywhere is not only liberating, it is inspiring, motivating, and comforting.

When in Dubai, I go for daily strolls (technically, rolls *ha ha*), either in my neighbourhood, or by the beach at the Jumeirah Beach Residence (JBR), without encountering a single step at times. All sidewalks are designed with ramps. These daily walks have been nourishment for my soul, a breath of fresh air which invigorates my whole being.

Dubai gives me the freedom to enjoy time with my family, just like the old days when I was healthy. With so many events happening all the time that are wheelchair accessible, who knows what I will be up to? One thing for sure is that I plan to take advantage of everything possible; life is too short to be wasted on hesitation to function. When I am there, I am so energised and enjoy spending time with my family, pampering them and being pampered by them.

*****

Life is a sequence of events. Some are joyful, some painful, some memorable and some we wish we could forget. But it is full of extraordinary moments that we must learn to treasure and appreciate. God let me live. He gave me an extension on my lease, for which I am eternally grateful, and so I feel obliged to make the most of it.

Being thankful in life is preached in every religion and one of the first lessons our parents teach us as children is to say "thank you" – it is one of the pillars of our foundation to becoming decent human beings.

I know most of us are grateful for so much, but we rarely stop to think, acknowledge, and appreciate what we are blessed with. Just look around you and try to identify things that life has enriched you with. Be thankful for being healthy, and for having a home to shelter you, and most importantly, be thankful for the unconditional love you give and receive from family and friends. I know I am despite the many challenges I am faced with.

*****

This is where this chapter was meant to end.

However, in the summer of 2020, after the first version of this book was written, I suffered a major setback to my health.

After enjoying years of stability, forgetting the dangers of ALS that loomed around me, 10 years after I lost my voice. I woke up one day feeling very tired and, out of the blue with no warning, my body started convulsing. The result of these violent tremors was a direct hit on my bulbar muscles, which are mainly responsible in helping me swallow and breathe. After that episode, I was unable to swallow most of my food, which led to rapid weight loss in only a few weeks – my weight went down to a measly 34 kg! As a result, my body was not regulating my breathing very well. In short, I was not taking in enough oxygen, and keeping in too much CO_2 – which was slowly poisoning me.

I was hospitalised and after lengthy consultations and discussions between my doctors, they came to the conclusion that I must undergo two major operations: one to install a feeding tube called a "PEG" tube, and the other was the long-dreaded tracheotomy: a breathing tube placed in my trachea to help me breathe. From then on, my life would forever be dependent on these machines – one for breathing, one for suction, and one to assist me in coughing. The doctors never warned me of the dark side effects that would wrack through my body. I lost my senses of smell and taste – it was the end of enjoying one of life's greatest pleasures: eating.

I was physically weak and had little hope in recovering from the devastating tracheotomy and adapting to the new way of life that came with it. I found myself full of self-doubt, self-pity, and fear. I was thinking, *This is the last limited time I have with my loved ones.* It was the darkest and hardest time of my life.

I was mentally weak – I had no desire to meditate, or to do reiki, which always used to help me. I felt defeated. For the first time, I felt that ALS had finally won the battle of survival. I longed for more time with my family. I found myself praying for comfort, and pain-free days and nights. I urged my body to fight back against the onslaught and discomfort of the continuous "suction" process (which gets rid of the secretions developing in my lungs due to the tracheotomy). I was broken and defeated. I begged for mercy from God and everyone around me.

Then, after two months of recovering from my operations and tremendous love and care from my amazing husband and family, my adorable granddaughter came to visit me. Just like that, it was as if a switch flicked on in my life, and a rainbow of hope and light was shining all around me. For the first time since my operations, I felt like I had a purpose to live again and go back to defeating ALS.

Seeing my granddaughter, Ghaia, smiling at me, touching me, and trying to communicate with me motivated me every single day. Her face served as a reminder of how much love I still have to give to my family, and miraculously I started to improve every single day. My mental state was in overdrive, I was hopeful again, I was optimistic, I was actually happy! I never thought I would say that word again a few months prior. This reflected favourably on my physical state as I started gaining weight again, my face was rosier, my eyes gained back the sparkle that shone with love.

Due to the PEG tube method of feeding, I am forced to eat only healthy smoothies and fresh fruits, which limits my intake to healthy options all the time. I have also resorted to sleeping and waking up early, thanks to my granddaughter's schedule, giving me a healthier lifestyle which in turn makes me happier and more relaxed throughout the day.

I am so grateful to be getting stronger and stronger every day. I gained more energy due to my healthy nourishment; this gives me the ability to enjoy more quality time with my lovely family.

I have gone back to appreciating my borrowed time with my loved ones, as opposed to those darkest days when I was convinced that I had run out of time.

I am so proud of myself for overcoming my obstacles, and believe me, they were not easy! It took every amount of strength and willpower I had.

Once again, love has proven to be the ultimate healer.

It's 5 am again, and the sun is gently pointing out that the party is over, go to bed, Zeid.

This wasn't a particularly special night, could have been a weekday, weekend, truth is I do not remember, which to me was the point. I smoked and drank way more than I will ever admit. Looking back at that party phase of my life, I think the excess was driven by two factors, 1) my age – early twenties, and 2) my family was going through an existential crisis and no one was talking about it. None of us knew how to deal with this situation, our mother, the nucleus of love in our family, was dying, slowly, and painfully, and there's nothing we can do to stop it.

I always thought I had time to discover the deeper mysteries of the universe, the big WHY and the purpose of it all. Life had other plans though, and shoved these questions to the forefront, I was now face-to-face with my own existential crises.

When I found out my mom has ALS, it was as if someone had flipped the hourglass of life, and death was racing down on our family. So, if I wanted to seriously make an attempt to discover the meaning of life, I better get to it. It is bitter sweet that our curiosity about the deepest secrets of our existence is often sparked by some sort of tragedy. We are all aware that bad things happen, but it is only when things go terribly wrong to us personally that that it flips from an abstract notion to a gross reality. A slow, painful, and unforgiving darkness was slowly inching towards us. Why is this happening to her? Why is this happening to us? There must be an answer to why? What does it all mean? There must be some wisdom in all of this, right? I kept repeating this to myself until I believed it. It was my only solace amongst a flood of dark thoughts. My lone candle in a dark cave.

The focus of my contemplation shifted from looking in the rear-view mirror to a bird's eye view of the whole thing. I came to realise that perspective shapes reality. I cannot overstate the importance of this realisation. The fact that we have control over our experience, is empowering beyond measure. The happiest and most loving people in life are not the ones whose circumstances are perfect, in fact, more often than not, it is the exact opposite. Khalil Gibran wrote "Out of suffering have emerged the strongest souls; the most massive characters are seared with scars." I pressed on with my daily yoga and meditation practice. I was in one particularly deep meditative state and a realisation dawned on me, that flipped my whole perspective right side up.

My mind was racing with memories of Loofy throughout my childhood, at home, at her shop, at school, at my sports games, at parties, in the car driving us back and forth, everywhere! I tried in vain to tell her many times that she does not need to attend every single game I play, or pick me up from every activity, but she would not listen. Loofy devoted her whole life to my brothers and I, and one particular phrase kept repeating throughout those flash flood of memories "Hayati", like a mantra, "Hayati", "Hayati inta", "Hayati inta" (Hayati or حياتي means "My Life" in Arabic). Loofy kept saying this phrase over and over. At the time it didn't seem like anything special, it was just mom being mom. She would sometimes follow it up with, "Hayati into, you'll never know how much I love you." It is no coincidence that this was her most repeated phrase to us, and the one that kept repeating in my head during this meditative experience. This fucked me up in the best way possible, tears were running down my cheeks. They were not tears of sadness, they were tears of relief. It was at that moment that I realised, Loofy knew, she knew it all along. Not consciously, but on a subconscious/ superconscious level, she knew. It explains all her behaviour, all her devotion, her mantra, "Hayati".

Mom could have spent her time doing a million other things. She had a big group of friends, she had many interests, she was very intelligent and very successful at every job she ever did, but she sacrificed it all to be with us. We were her life, we are her life, she is our life, we are life to each other... bonded by the deepest love. Love that transcends both time and space.

There is no adequate mix of words or emotions that can capture a feeling of understanding, it can only be felt. From that day on, my perspective on the Loofy experience feels more like cosmic feedback loop. My soul was introduced to this life through Loofy, Loofy's soul found meaning through her love for us, later I found meaning through my love for her. At this point, this love is literally keeping her alive. This cosmic love dance has no beginning and no end.

What appears to have happened before or after, Mom's love and devotion to us, or our love and devotion to her, is irrelevant, they both currently exist, right now. And this is the meaning I have found that makes sense. Love happened, and this is where we are. We chose love, and it is because of that we are here today. My teacher once said, "The measure of your intelligence is your ability to love." Makes sense to me. In a fleeting and impermanent existence, what is better than to be in love? This is the meaning we choose to live by today, to find love in all things at all times.

Recently my wife and I were blessed with our first child. Just when we thought we understood love, the universe opens the door to a brand-new dimension of infinite love. We live our day to day lives as mindfully as possible, cherishing all the small things, because we know this experience will not last forever. We will all die someday, this is the only guarantee in life, so it makes no sense to fear it or ignore it. Right now, though, we are alive, man! We choose love over fear, we choose our story to be a love story.

It's 5am again, and the dawn of a new day is slowly spreading light across the sky, time to wake up, Zeid.

– **Zeid Bataineh,** Lana's eldest son.

Growth

When I was delivered the devastating news of my ALS diagnosis, I went through all the negative feelings you can imagine: fear, frustration, denial, anger, helplessness, sadness, and despair. I went through these waves of emotions in various degrees until one day, amidst my mixture of self-pity, heartache, and hidden tears, emerged a new positive feeling; a feeling that delivered itself to me out of necessity: hope.

Hope is one of the strongest four-letter words in the English language. It can heal the sick, revive the broken spirit, nourish the soul, and make the impossible possible. Without hope in all aspects of our life, we might as well give up and admit defeat from the word "go".

Hope is when you think you are drowning at the bottom of the ocean then you see someone or something rescuing you. I was drowning in my dark thoughts when, suddenly, I looked up and saw my children. I felt an unbelievable desire to be saved, for their sake as much as for mine. That is when my body was taken over by a higher power; the power of hope. I felt that if I wanted to survive strongly enough then it would happen. One of my favourite quotes, which I think applies to my situation, is the saying by Elna Rae, *"Where hope grows, miracles blossom."*

Hope was born inside me when I started praying to be saved, praying to be cured, believing in my prayers and trusting that my faith can defy science. Medicine and doctors keep telling us, ALS patients, that there is no cure. But research, and hope, are telling me a different story. Hope is telling me that research and trials are constantly being conducted all over the world. I choose to listen to the latter and be hopeful. It is a choice that has proven to be life changing, for myself and my family.

Hope has become my best friend, my companion, my mantra that I keep repeating to myself. As well as my motivational word that fuels my fire to get through my days. I am hopeful that, someday, they will find a cure for ALS. I am also hopeful that my strong will to stay alive and my love for my family will yield a miracle. I am living proof of the Elna Rae words. The mere fact I am surviving and thriving is a miracle.

Hope and positive thoughts have a power: if sent out to the universe, the universe will respond favourably. If you are going through a rough period in your life, or if a loved one is suffering in any shape or form, try hope. It does not cost anything, and you have nothing to lose, trust me.

Often times, fellow ALS patients and their caregivers ask me for advice. From my experience, here is what I can share so far. When I was first diagnosed, I came across an amazing neuro physiotherapist who explained to me, in detail, the importance of preserving what muscles I have left that are yet to be affected by this disease. He explained that by gently exercising, massaging, and using these muscles, I could ensure their longevity. Basically, label your body: "Fragile: handle with care".

I also taught myself to preserve my energy prior to and after any activity or outing; that way, I lessen the possibility of further muscle decay. I allocated a time for a daily nap every afternoon, and I make sure to adhere to it no matter what is happening. Everyone in my surrounding circle has learnt to accept that and work around it – rest is vital for our (ALS patients') survival. I also make sure that I do my 15 minutes of physio twice a day, every single day, to ensure flexibility and elasticity. I love the saying by Jon Kabat Zinn, "*You can't stop the waves, but you can learn to surf.*"

Perhaps the strongest weapon you can have is to surround yourself with loved ones; fill your life with precious sentimental possessions, motivational quotes, and people that bring happiness into your heart. For love has proven to be the miracle healing drug. It motivates and empowers your thoughts to remain hopeful. Love gives you a purpose to persevere and fight to take back your life.

I stay away as much as I can from negativity. That means news mainly, which is constantly so negative. I do not mean to live like an ostrich with your head in the sand, *ha ha*, I just do not keep listening and watching horrific news. Listen to headlines to catch up on current events, and then move on. For example, I watch comedy, quiz shows, and sports; I do not dwell on negative news.

Doctors are not always right, science is not always right, statistics are just numbers. Each human being is unique, and each patient is different. We react differently to medications, we handle situations differently, and therefore our life expectancy is not the same. Just remember these facts every single day, send out your hopes and dreams to the universe and you will be pleasantly surprised how many wishes come true.

Another coping mechanism I use for dealing with ALS is setting goals for myself and using them as stepping stones to navigate my way through turbulent times. In order to achieve your goals, you must dream and have the desire and determination to turn them into a reality.

When I first got sick, I was worried that I would not be there to witness my youngest graduate from school, so I set it as my first goal. The day Karim graduated I was ecstatic and went on to set a new goal for myself, and an ambitious one to say the least (at least it felt so at the time): I wanted to be there for my boys' university graduations. I would put this image in my mind, visualise it, feel it, pray for it, and be determined to make that dream come true, until it did. I dream just like any mother to see my children succeed in life, excel in their work and be happy. I promised myself that I have to be alive to witness their accomplishments.

After achieving my goals one after the other, I started asking myself "dare I dream of attending their weddings?" The answer was and still is, yes! I visualised the day my first-born would get married, I dreamt of all the details, and it all came true. Now that that dream became a reality, I have set myself a new goal: to plan and experience the weddings of my other two boys – and hopefully see them both happily married, just like their older brother.

I make a point of setting new goals as soon as I accomplish each checkpoint. Reaching my target fills me with strength, which, in turn, propels me to keep persevering and riding the euphoric wave of success onto my new, courageous adventure.

As I keep setting new targets, hopes, dreams, and ways to accomplish these goals, life inevitably becomes rosier, and much more optimistic.

*****

For me, it is like somehow God was looking out for me and my children, as if I knew I had limited time to spend with them, (of course I had no idea). When they were young, thankfully, I spent maximum quality time with them.

My greatest pleasure was attending every single sports game they played, whether in Little League, school games, or national club championships. I was there cheering them on and enjoying every minute of it. My sons were three competitive athletes so they took up most of my time. Driving them to practice or games was our special bonding time. I would hear all about their life in school, their friends, their worries, fears, and joys. We would laugh together and I would deliver my values, discipline, and motherly advice to them.

A little extra time is what I needed, hoped, and prayed for, in order to spend time with my youngest, Karim, before I got sick. I needed a couple more years to be there for him and guide him through his teenage years as I had done for his brothers. Instead of running all over the world – from London, to the US, to Pakistan, and China – trying to find a cure for my diagnosis. I would have loved to prepare him for his university life, but things do not always go as planned, time was stolen away from me.

Today, I am blessed to be living on very valuable borrowed time. After the doctors told me in 2004 to get my affairs in order, I thought I was racing against the clock; but again, God had other plans for me, *Hamdallah*. He gave me the gift of time. Time to appreciate life, to spend with my family, to love and be loved, to laugh and be happy, and time to be hopeful and thankful.

That is why now I am always the optimistic one. The extended time I am enjoying now is the result of my faith and love from my extremely supportive family. I get to look back and appreciate time and be grateful for every extra day that comes my way. I plan on turning my days into weeks, months, and years for maximum time with my loved ones.

One of the greatest blessings that came out of my illness is that my family and I learnt how to live in the moment. When my doctors practically assured us that tomorrow was no longer ours to share, that yesterday was just memories, and that all we had was now, we made sure we treasured every hour given to us. We learnt how to appreciate and value our time together. This carried forward into my family's day-to-day life. As a family, we always search for the blessings in disguise in whatever situation we are put in. In the words of Maya Angelou, "*God put rainbows in the clouds.*"

My ALS taught us a valuable lesson in life: treasure every moment with your loved ones, for tomorrow may never come. Living in the moment means giving 100% of yourself to the people you are with, and in return you are receiving 100% of their attention. Living in the moment can be as simple as looking out of a window while drinking coffee or taking a shower. It can also be as adventurous as discovering somewhere new, or going on a safari. What matters is focusing on the task at hand, and soaking up the beauty around you and making every minute of your life count for something or someone.

After being deprived of the freedom to roam around on this earth, I have learned to appreciate whatever I see. Things I used to take for granted, I now learned to appreciate the natural beauty found in them. Like the trees, flowers, grass, or even a visit to a park. I have learned to look at the colours available in nature, which I never used to see before. So many shades of green and yellow. I see the world much more beautifully than I used to. Seeing beauty in my surroundings automatically boosts my mood and spirit, creating a positive outlook for my world.

***** .

Our lives are full of choices and we spend all day making decisions. Sometimes they are trivial, like "do you like your coffee with milk?" or "Sugar with your tea?" Sometimes we are forced to make more decisive choices like what to wear, what to eat, where to go... etc. Then there are the more important choices, like what to study, where to apply for work, decisions concerning our family and so on.

Making the right choices on how we want to live will end up being the blueprint of our lives. Hence it is only fitting that we aim to make the right ones in order to enrich our lives with the quality of our decisions.

If we choose to be happy instead of miserable, imagine how wonderful life would be and how happy and serene our life would become. So simple, yet so profound. I personally made the ultimate decision, when I was struck by ALS, to choose life over defeat. I chose to survive and thrive instead of surrender. Those choices have helped me remain a loving doting mother to my children till this day and, hopefully, for many more to come.

Unconditional love is the love for our children, spouse, or parent which is so fulfilling, precious, and dear to our hearts. We love them no matter what, despite their flaws. Unconditional happiness is waking up and making a conscious choice to be happy, despite what events might go wrong during the day, or during the course of our life. Let's face it, there will be days when things will go wrong, or someone will upset us – that is all part of being alive. If we stay true to our choices then our level of happiness will peak, no matter what happens.

I made a choice to be unconditionally happy despite my very difficult situation, and despite the hardships I endure on a daily basis. Believe it or not, I am a very happy patient. Of course, there are days when I get extremely upset from someone or something; I am human after all. But the trick is that I remind myself of my choice. So, I snap out of my misery, and find myself having an enjoyable day. Being happy is a conscious choice I made. Just like the marriage vows, "For better or worse, in sickness and in health, for richer or for poorer", this is a commitment. I promised myself to maintain my sanity and my zest for life.

The great thing about this decision is that it also spreads to my family members. Hopefully, they will be encouraged to make more positive choices in their lives too, having seen their mother lead by example.

There is a saying: *"When one door closes, another opens."* This holds true for me in so many ways. ALS has closed many doors on me, from walking to talking, but I have always stayed positive and looked for an open door. Despair should never be the answer, we should always try to find a way out, no matter how serious the problem we are facing is.

It is important to accept our situation, before we can attempt to find a solution. Finding an alternative can be just under our nose, but if we refuse to acknowledge our problem, and accept that we are facing a closed door, then there is no way we will see it.

Eating, drinking, sleeping, and breathing are all basic activities which most of us take for granted, but for me it is a minefield that I have to navigate through. One that compels me to seek open doors that will facilitate my journey in life. It is an on-going process that requires acceptance, resilience, and perseverance.

I continue to face some struggles in my daily life, but I do not let them weigh me down, I concentrate on the solution, not the problem.

I choose love.

For no apparent reason, Lana almost tripped while crossing Times Square on a beautiful New York evening in late August 2004. "Mom, that was clumsy," our son said, or was it, "you are running funny," I cannot remember now; but that is how it started. Two months later, the doctors confirmed it was ALS.

It is hard to imagine how three letters can change your life forever. I do not want to chronicle Lana's history fighting ALS, rather I want to remember her as she was and what motivates her to keep fighting and waking up every morning full of life, hope, and determination. I want to tell how she inspires all around her and how she has found new meaning to her own life and maybe to life in general.

Someone once told me that everything happens for a reason, I thought then that I understood what they meant. I realise now that I did not, but I do now. I do not believe that HE is testing us or punishing us, HE is not that ruthless. However, I do believe that there are other forms of living, other meanings to our existence, other ways to serve one's time on earth, our life sentence if you wish. And I am not just talking about Lana, but also about me, about Zeid and Faisal and Karim.

Each one of us found his own way to live. Lana has been organised and disciplined since she came to this earth, my attempts to change her notwithstanding. You see, everything happens for a reason. It is her love of life, but above all, it is her discipline that is making all the difference, and allowing her to retain control of her life and maintain her sanity. But her single strongest driver is her sons. She is determined to see them grow up, graduate, work, get married, and see their children. Her expectations are a moving target. At the beginning, she was content with high school graduation, now after so many years of living with ALS she is not afraid to hope for more.

I sometimes feel sorry for me. I am not coping as well as Lana. This sounds crazy, unreal, but it is true. Her case is clear: black and white. While I am not sure what my role should be. I mean beyond the expected or the conventional, is my life reduced to a supporting cast? Is that all I can do? Should I do more? Do I have a life of my own anymore? Should I? Am I being a selfish callous brute for wanting that?

The truth is, as time goes by, I admire Lana more. I see qualities that I wished I had: the discipline, the clear mind, the absolute dedication to the task at hand, the unwavering resolve to make whatever time she has left meaningful and good for the children, her love of living. This may sound bizarre; who would want to live like this? But she can see beyond her physical limitations; her job as a mother is not finished.

Just look at her daily routine: she wakes up between 9:30 and 9:45 every morning like clockwork. After bathroom she watches television and has breakfast until 10:45. Then 15–20 minutes morning exercises in bed after her bath. By then, it is almost noon; office hours. She sits on Eyegaze, checking and answering emails and giving instructions to the staff. Some days she receives guests. Lunch at 2pm, then afternoon nap until 5:30, followed by her evening exercises in bed. Visitors between 6 and 8, dinner at 9, then watches TV till 11:30, bed time. Next day same thing all over again. It may sound monotonous, far from it.

Every day there is something happening: checking house needs, the rooms, buying furniture, gifts, new recipes for meals and sweets, keeping in touch with family and friends' news and all the gossip in Bahrain and Amman, doing her Reiki and energy healing sessions... Her life is not boring.

Lana has been living with ALS for over 16 years now and she is still thriving, thank God. Her perseverance paid off. All of our three sons graduated from university, working and prospering. Zeid got married to the most wonderful girl,

Reem, and God blessed us with the most precious gift: a baby girl. Ghaia has brought so much joy and happiness and new meaning to our lives, especially to Lana's.

Time may not heal everything, but it certainly blunts the emotions and makes you more tolerant and accepting. It teaches you how to reorganise and prioritise your life. All the family learned how to cope with the new normal, our life simply revolves around Lana; to ensure her comfort and well-being in everything we do. Lana always tries to put a positive spin on every situation, but I know that her life is a constant struggle; even the simplest thing like communicating her basic needs takes effort and energy, so we endeavour to make sure that her life is not even more difficult.

Lana keeps moving the goalpost; as soon as a milestone is achieved, she sets a new one.

It would be wrong to assume that Lana simply exists to look after us and plan for her family and her home, she keeps afloat of events and developments in her wider circle of friends and acquaintances, her charities, as well as national and global news. Lana is a fighter who never lost hope for a cure; always on the lookout for the latest ALS research, new medications and developments in fighting this disease.

Lana is prospering and sticking around until all her wishes have come true. My admiration and love for her keep growing.

– **Marwan Bataineh**, Lana's loving and devoted husband